The Journey of Kathak

In conversation with Dr. Puru Dadheech - Part I

Kiran Java

Copyright © 2023 Kiran Java

Cover Photo by: Tush Dadheech

All rights reserved

No part of this book may be reproduced, or stored in a retrieval system, or transmitted in any form or by any means, electronic, mechanical, photocopying, recording, or otherwise, without express written permission of the publisher.

*To my family and friends who are always
supportive of my endless pursuits.*

Those who are intelligent cut through the binding knots of
karma with the sword of the Lord's remembrance.

Who then will not pay attention to His katha!

BHAGAVATA PURANA 1.2.15

Contents

Title Page
Copyright
Dedication
Epigraph
About the Cover Photo
Preface
Prologue by Kiran Java — 1
Origin of dance — 8
Dance in the ancient period — 15
Dance and Kathak — 18
Origin of the word Kathak — 26
Descent of Drama on Earth — 31
Development of Kathak as a community — 35
Journey of Kathak — 39
Epilogue by Kiran Java — 43
Reference Shlokas — 51
Shloka - Mahabharata — 52
Shloka - Origin of dance — 54

Shloka - Descent of Drama on Earth	56
Shloka - Occasions for dance	57
Shloka - Sangeet Ratnakar	59
Shloka - Harshacharitam	60
Shloka - Prakrit verse	62
Shloka - Constant Prayoga	64
Reference - Amarakosha	66
Reference - Kalpadruma	67
Books By This Author	69
About The Author	71

About the Cover Photo

Dr. Puru Dadheech narrates a poetry piece at the Ravindra Natya Mandir, Mumbai on the occasion of the convocation of Natyashastra with Kathak relevancy course organized by Bharata College of Fine Arts & Culture.

The cover photo was taken by Tush Dadheech, son of Mahamahopadhyaya Dr. Puru Dadheech, who has successfully brought the story of the Kathak legends to the *rasikas* and students alike. Tush is also an ace photographer, publicist and artist manager.

His exceptional work can be viewed on his Instagram profile tushdadeechphotography.

Preface

Conversations with Mahamahopadhyaya Dr. Puru Dadheech are always fascinating, enlightening and full of wisdom. He is a charming, intelligent and seasoned connoisseur in a diverse array of art forms and disciplines. With over six decades of experience in both theory and practise of Kathak classical dance, Dr. Dadheech is renowned as an educator, Sanskrit expert, and author. He has received the Padma Awards, Kalidas Samman, Tagore Fellowship, Sangeet Natak Akademi, and other honours for his contributions to Kathak classical dance and the performing arts.

I was introduced to the writings of Dr. Puru Dadheech when I began learning Kathak under Dr. Nandkishore Kapote. He recommended many books authored by Dr. Puru Dadheech to deepen my understanding of the theory of Kathak classical dance.

Later, I studied the Natyashastra with Kathak relevancy under Dr. Puru Dadheech and a new perspective on performing arts was revealed to me. The many long discussions with Dr. Puru Dadheech about the history of Kathak revealed new facets of the journey.

In this book, we explore the history and journey of Kathak classical dance through conversations with Dr. Puru Dadheech. He clarifies pertinent questions and dispels myths about this beautiful art form, providing us with a unique and insightful perspective.

Happy reading!

Best wishes,

Kiran Java

www.kiranjava.com

Prologue by Kiran Java

*K*atha has been defined in a number of ways. Macdonell defines it as a 'conversation', while Monier Williams Cologne defines it as a 'discussion', Vaman Shivaram Apte as 'an account', Benfey as a 'tale', and Amarakosh as '*prabandh-kalpana* or 'imaginative essays'.

Katha is also used to refer to a 'philosophical debate,' which appears later in the Chandogya Upanishad.

Another unique perspective of *Katha* that I heard was in a presentation by Ph.D. research scholar and Mumbai University faculty Kanakavalli S. Chari. She linked *Katha* in association with *Yagna* in the Vedas. These were rituals that took place over days at a time and the participants of *yagnas* performed the rituals from sunrise to sunset.

The evenings were the community's collective free time. Sutas, or travelling storytellers, engaged the community by sharing stories about the culture of the time, exchanging socio-cultural ideas, and providing collective counselling. This elevated the storytelling experience by transporting the audience to a world of narrative, relatable situations and providing them with valuable lessons to take away.

A similar perspective of Katha and performance is in an article published in a journal by the Sangeet

Natak Akdemi. In his article, Harikatha: Origin, Growth and Purpose, published in Sangeet Natak, Volume XLII, number 2, 2008, Balameera Chandra writes,

"Spiritual story- telling in India has been in existence from the Vedic period. During the intervals between Vedic rituals, stories from the Upanisads were narrated for the benefit of the people. This was called Akhyana. The story of Rama, i.e., the Ramayana was sung by Lav and Kush with accompaniments during the ritual performed by Rama. The Puranas, which are the storehouse of stories of the gods and goddesses, were recited and expounded for a long time in various ways: Purana Patanam is the reading and

expounding of the spiritual text. Pravacanam is the way of story-telling in which the text will be sung to a minimum of musical notes. Upanyasam is another version of pravacanam that includes side stories (upakathas) and philosophical explanations. Thus we can see that the art of story-telling with music is an age-old activity in India."

In a recent presentation by Prof. Gauri Mahulikar, I saw another interesting interpretation of *Katha* where she splits the word *Katha* into two - 'Ka' and 'Tha'. The two words denote - How did it (such and such episode) take place and what happened.

In my view, *Katha* is an exploration of the lifestyle and culture of a specific group of people within a particular time and place. *Katha* provides a window into a culture through its stories. The performing arts breathe life into these tales, bringing the stories of *Katha* to life.

A unique tradition of amalgamation of the performing arts with *Katha* can be seen in the 'Araiyar Ganam' tradition, also called 'Araiyar Sevai'. In the ninth and tenth centuries, the revered scholar Nathamuni rediscovered the lost verses to the Lord known as *Divya Prabandams*. He set them to music and created accompanying *abhinaya* gestures for them so that they could be performed and passed down in the oral tradition through generations. He taught his nephews Melagathazhwan and Kizhagathazhwan what he had discovered including the musical arrangments and choreography. This was the beginning of the Araiyar Tradition which continues till this day.

An interesting exposition on this tradition can be found in an article by Suganthy Krishnamachari, published in The Hindu on September 01, 2016. In her article she writes,

'In Ramanuja's time, Araiyars were called isaikaarar —musicians, indicating that their music and dance had been recognised as a profession. Ramanuja institutionalised Araiyar Sevai, which conforms to the definition of music as given by Sarngadeva in Sangita Ratnakara: "Geetam vadyam tatha nrityam, trayam sangitamuchyate" — vocal music, instrumental

music and dance together constitute music. Araiyars sing, dance and keep beat with a pair of cymbals.'

The Performing arts take *katha* stories a step further by bringing to life salient nuances that cannot be expressed in words. Thus a happy symbiotic relationship between both *Katha* and the performing arts can be seen.

Origin of dance

Since time immemorial, the art of dance has flourished in the Indian ethos. The rich history of dance in Indian culture dates back to ancient times and is deeply rooted in the Natyashastra.This text, believed to have been written between 200 BC and 200 AD (or possibly 500 BC to 500 AD), is attributed to Sage Bharata Muni and outlines the theories and practices of performing arts, including dance.

Dance has always been a natural expression of joy and happiness, and humans are born with the innate ability to move rhythmically with beat and tempo.

When a dance has structured codified movements as prescribed by the Natyashastra, it is referred to as a classical dance.

The Natyashastra recounts the story of the origin of dance. The story begins in the days of yore when the golden Age (*Satyuga*) ended with the reign of Svayambhuva Manu, and the Silver Age (*Tretayuga*) commenced under Vaivasvata Manu. During that period people became addicted to sensual pleasures and were swayed by desire, greed, jealousy and anger. Indra and the other gods approached Brahma and requested an audible and visual diversion from him.

Brahma agreed and created a fifth Veda with

itihasas (such as the Mahabharata and others) to remind people of *Dharma* and *Artha,* to guide them, and to explain the arts and crafts.

He took recitation (*pathya*) from the Rigveda, song from the Samaveda, Histrionic Representation (*abhinaya*) from the Yajurveda, and Sentiments (*rasa*) from the Atharvaveda. As a result, the Natyaveda was born.

Brahma created *itihasas* and requested that Indra give it to the gods to dramatise. Indra stated that the gods are incapable of performing these dramas and that this art must be preserved. Brahma then instructed Sage Bharata to use Natyaveda with his sons.

Bharata Muni wrote a play in several dramatic

styles, including *Bharati, Sattvati,* and *Arabhati.* Brahma then requested that he incorporate the *Kaisiki,* or gentle, style into the production.

Bharata Muni responded by saying that he had seen Shiva perform the *Kaisiki* style, which is very graceful. It needed beautiful dresses and the movements had gentle *angharas, rasas,* and *bhavas* that are appropriate for the *Shringara* sentiment. He asked Brahma to supply him appropriate materials. He also said that men could not perform this without the help of women.

Brahma then created Apsaras from his mind, who were skilled at enhancing drama and asked them to assist Bharata Muni in his performances. Svati and his disciples played the musical instruments.

He asked Narada and other Gandharvas to sing the songs.

Brahma was pleased and asked Sage Bharata to stage a play on the occasion of the 'Banner Festival' of Indra. The play was successful and the Gods were pleased.

The *daityas* however were extremely unhappy as the play portrayed their race in a bad light and they created havoc. Brahma had to manage to console them.

Later Brahma asked Sage Bharata to write and perform a play (drama) for Lord Shiva. The Natyashastra describes 'Drama' as:

'Stories taken out of the Vedic lore as well as Semi-historical Tales, capable of giving pleasure.'

Bharata Muni performed the 'Amruta-Manthana, the Churning of the Ocean', a *Samavakara* class play, and the 'Tripuradaha, the Burning of Tripura', a *Dima* class play. Shiva was pleased with the drama put on by Bharata's group. He asked him to include dance in the *purvaranga*, the beginning of the play.

Shiva said,

"Now in the evening, while performing it, I remembered that dance made beautiful by Angaharas consisting of different Karanas. You may utilize these in the Preliminaries (purvaranga) of a play."

Shiva then appointed Tandu to teach Bharata the nuances of dance. Because it was taught by Tandu the dance was called 'Tandava'. This was the beginning of dance according to the Natyashastra.

Dance in the ancient period

Classical dance has evolved over time and is now categorized into specific styles such as Bharatnatyam, Odissi, Kathakali, and others. These names refer to the *'shailee'* or style of dance. The Sangeet Natak Academy recognizes eight classical dances in India – Bharatanatyam, Kathak, Kuchipudi, Odissi, Kathakali, Sattriya, Manipuri, and Mohiniyattam. The classical dance 'style' of North India, for example, is known as Kathak. But it wasn't always this way.

The development of these specific styles was a result of cultural and regional influences, as well as historical events, which shaped the dance form into what it is today. These classical dance styles are not only rich in cultural heritage but are also a testament to the evolution of the art of dance in India.

There is an entire chapter dedicated to dance in most ancient music treatises. The name of this chapter is simply termed *'Nritya adhyaya'*, which means chapter concerning dance. There is a detailed description of *'Nritya'* in this chapter, but there are no names for the styles associated with dance.

In fact, at first, no names were assigned to the various styles. It's worth noting that dance was named after the subject it revolved around or portrayed.

The beautiful *shringarik* dance of Krishna and Gopis in the mood of *Bhakti* or devotion, for example, was dubbed *Raas.* Similarly, a dance to Dhrupad music was simply referred to as Dhrupad. A dance on a specific *Taal,* say *Roopak Taal*, was simply referred to as '*Roopak Taal Nritya.*'

Dance and Kathak

In the early 20th century, a conversation took place around 1935-1936, focused on establishing standardized terms for the various styles of dance in India. The objective of this discussion was to officially recognize and categorize dance based on its distinct characteristics and cultural origins. The outcome of this discussion resulted in the official naming of the different styles of dance, which helped to preserve and promote the rich heritage of Indian classical dance.

The Devadasis of South India, who had a rich tradition of performing in temples to pay homage to the gods through their art, referred to their dance as Dasiattam or Sadir. Another name for the classical dance in South India was Tanjore Nritya, as it originated in the city of Tanjore or Mysore.

The dance form was later revived and named Bharatnatyam by Rukmini Arundale (1904 - 1986), an Indian theosophist, dancer, and choreographer of Indian classical dance. It was said that Bharata was represented by Bha meaning Bhava, Ra meaning Raaga, and Ta meaning Taala. It was a cross between Bhava, Raaga, and Taala. And hence Bharatanatyam was chosen as the name for the dance.

∞∞∞

Note by the author:

In the Times of India an article '*The reinvention of dance: From Sadir to Bharatanatyam*' dated February 12, 2016 states:

Krishna Iyer was the cause for Bharatanatyam to become "an art of every household". Thereby dance was able to shed the disgraceful shroud it was covered with and became a popular art form that could be learned and practiced. His caliber can be known from the fact that when he was arrested by the British, he met with leaders in prison and convinced many of them of the urgent need to revive dance. Being at the helm of affairs at the Music Academy, as its founder, he actually sought and did remove the stigma that was attached to Sadir. He glorified it and rechristened it by passing the 1932 resolution to name it Bharatanatyam.

Thus In 1932, E Krishna Iyer and Rukmini Devi Arundale put forward a proposal to rename Sadiraattam, also known as Parathaiyar Aattam or Thevarattam, as "Bharatanatyam", at a meeting of the Madras Music Academy.

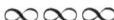

Other dance revivalists named their respective dances in a similar manner. The name Kathakali was coined by Maha Kavi Vallathol Narayana Menon (1878-1958), who is best known for reviving Kathakali in Kerala. The name Manipuri was coined by Ravindranath Thakur for the Manipur dance.

The term Kathak was first applied to Kathak dance in the 1930s. It was in July 1926 that Pt. Vishnu Narayan Bhatkhande founded the Bhatkhande Music Institute University, formerly known as the Marris College of Hindustani Music.

Ramdutt Mishra, Shambhu Maharaj's maternal uncle and the doyen of the Lucknow Gharana of Kathak, was assigned to teach dance at this institute. At the same institute another dance instructor taught Bharatnatyam. When they were asked what the name of their respective dance styles would be called, the teacher teaching Bharatnatyam said his dance is called Bharatnatyam. Ramdutt Mishra said that since he belonged to the Kathak community, his dance style should be called Kathak

Nritya.

Thus Kathak was coined as the name for what we know today as Kathak classical dance.

∞∞∞

Note by the author:

Instances of the word Kathak being used to describe this dance style for the first time can be found in the following references.

Reference 1:

Dated: 1937

On March 15th, 1937, the Hindustan Times newspaper published an article titled "The Kathak School of Indian Dancing," which highlights two important points for the purposes of this discussion.

Zutski describes a performance style similar to today's Kathak and, asserts that this school is in the hands of a community of Brahmans who are called "Kathaks".

This supports the notion that there was, in fact, a community called Kathak.

"It also appears that the dance was first referred to as "Kathak" in the 1930s." In 1937, Zutshi referred to the art he was describing as "the Kathak style (or school) of dance"

This supports the notion that the dance was called Kathak style of dance.

Reference 2:

Dated 1939

"Dancing in India," an article published in Indian Art and Letters in 1939, describes a lecture-demonstration given by American dancer Russell Meriweather Hughes, who performed and published under the name La Meri, and simply referred to this dance as "Kathak" in her article.

(See: Margaret Edith Walker's 2004 thesis, Kathak, a Critical History)

Origin of the word Kathak

Kathak, the word and the tradition can be traced back to ancient India and is referenced in two of the most famous Hindu epics, the Mahabharata and the Ramayana. The Mahabharata was compiled between the 3rd century BC and the 3rd century AD and the Ramayana is believed to have been compiled between the 7th and 4th century BC. These references to Kathak in ancient texts provide a glimpse into the long-standing tradition and cultural significance of this classical dance form in India.

Over the centuries, Kathak has evolved and adapted to changing times, but its basic elements have remained unchanged, reflecting its historical roots and cultural heritage.

The shloka in the Mahabharata from the Nritya Nibandh by Dr. Puru Dadheech and Dr. Vibha Dadheech is below:

kathakAshachApare rAjan shramanasha cha vanaukasa: (1/251/3) (Adiparva)

The Sabdakalpadruma (An Encyclopaedic Dictionary of Sanskrit Words), the well-known Sanskrit lexicon, contains the words 'Kushi-Luv'. Kushilav refers to those who spread the teachings of the shastras.

In the Ramayana, Luv and Kush are Lord Ram's twin sons who grow up in Sage Valmiki's ashram. Valmiki is known to be *'tri-kaal darshi,'* meaning he could see into the past, present, and future. He is known to have written the incidents of the Ramayana before Lord Ram was born. He had taught the Ramayana to Luv and Kush at the ashram.

Ram returned to Ayodhya and performed the *'Ashvamedha yagna'* ritual, which involved leaving a horse to wander for a year. Anyone could challenge the king's authority by fighting the warriors who accompanied the horse. When Ram's horse wandered into Valmiki's ashram, the twin boys caught hold of it. They went to Ram's court in Ayodhya and sang the Ramayana with song and *abhinaya* (gestures). Ram recognized them as his sons and appointed them as heirs to his kingdom. As a result, they became the princes of Ayodhya.

This tradition of singing and acting out the Ramayana in memory of Luv and Kush was carried on by other residents of the land. Those who made this their living became known as 'Kushiluv'.

According to the Kalpadruma (Sanskrit Lexicon), the *'vritti'* or profession of the 'Kushiluv' is to sing the Ramayana while performing *abhinaya* or gestures.

The first Kathak was performed by Sage Valmiki, and the tradition has since continued. Professions in our country, India, span generations and continue within families. Traditionally, sons take up their father's profession. This is how the Kushilav tradition was preserved.

Descent of Drama on Earth

The story of dance descending to Earth is a significant event in the history of classical dance in India and is described in the Natyashastra, a text attributed to Sage Bharata Muni. According to the text, the Natyashastra, Shiva had asked for dance to be incorporated in the Purvaranga or preliminaries of the drama. However, the gods and goddesses in the heavens were the only ones who could enjoy the beauty and elegance of dance. Dance was only performed in the heavens *(swarga)* and had not yet arrived on Earth.

When Raja Nahush was appointed as the next

Indra, he had access to the heavens. He heard the beautiful music of the Gandharvas and saw the dances of the Apsaras and wished that his palace on earth would also have this performing art. He requested the *Devas* if they could send them to dance in his palace on earth. But they refused as Gandharvas and Apsaras were heavenly beings and would not descend on Earth to live. They encouraged Raja Nahush to consult with Sage Bharata.

Raja Nahush told Sage Bharata that during the time of his grandfather Pururuvas, Urvashi had taught performing arts to many citizens in the palace. But tragedy struck when Urvashi left for the heavens and Pururavas died of a broken heart. The citizens were so distraught that they forgot all about dance and drama. Raja Nahush requested Bharata Muni if he could once again revive dance and drama on Earth.

Sage Bharata did not want to turn down the kind King's request. He then had the idea of sending his sons to earth because they had been cursed by the sages and that way they could be freed from their curse.

He sent his sons to Earth to spread the performing arts. They married and had children with earthly women. They taught their children the performing arts and produced numerous plays and dramas on Earth.

Thus dance was brought down to Earth, allowing

humans to experience its beauty and grace. The Natyashastra describes this event as the birth of classical dance on Earth.

Development of Kathak as a community

Bharata Muni's descendants, who were highly skilled in the performing arts, continued to propagate the art form on Earth. The tradition of performing arts was passed down from generation to generation. As the descendants of Bharata Muni flourished, they continued to develop the various aspects of classical dance, including movements, postures, and expressions. They also created new forms of dance and added new elements to existing styles, making the art form more diverse and dynamic.

The Amarkosh, one of the oldest extant Sanskrit lexicons, mentions various *'jaatis'* (classes) of people performing 'Nat' and 'Nritya' actions (*karmas*). These classes are denoted as

Shilalin, Shailush (Vedic dancers), Jayajeev (those living off the earnings of their wives), Krishashvin, Bharat, Kushiluv, and Charanas.

The Kushiluv were known for their exceptional musical abilities and thus were included in the musical ensemble of Bharata's theatrical performances. Over time, they also found opportunities to act in various character roles in these plays. As noted in the works of influential scholars like Chanakya and Vatsayana, the Kushiluv were often invited to perform in character roles during major festival celebrations.

The Kushiluv initially performed the Ramayana, then after the Dwapur Yuga, they moved on to performing the *leela* plays of Lord Krishna. Later they performed story plays from various other Puranas.

As they continued to propagate these stories through song and gestures, they came to be known as 'Kathak', or those who perform Katha. They made this their tradtional vocation. This eventually led to the formation of a distinct Kathak community, particularly in Uttar Pradesh.

Through song and *abhinaya*-gestures they performed these kathas from village to village and in temple courtyards.

Journey of Kathak

In exploring the evolution of Kathak, it's helpful to divide the evolution into two time periods. The first encompasses the period from the start of time to the 10th century, while the second covers the period from the 10th century to the present. This discussion focuses on the first time period.

During this time, the tradition of storytelling and performance was closely tied to the practice of *Yagna* fire sacrifices, dating back to the Vedic period. The emergence of the Kushilavs and those involved in singing, dancing, and music also took place during this time, marking the rise of the arts in general.

In the early days of dance, music was not divided into two streams of North and South, rather the art of dance grew into two distinct streams that evolved side by side.

One form was for a divine purpose - dancing for glorifying the Lord as a part of *Bhakti marg* or path of devotion. The other stream was for a more mundane and worldly purpose. During that ancient period, we see certain distinct characteristics.

Members of the community (Kushiluvs and others) taught dance to princesses, queens, and wives of rich merchants and feudal lords who were patrons of their music schools.

Kushilav and others joined a temple or monastery and trained the Devadasis and played the role of their accompanists. Additionally, they become teachers and mentors of the 'Varanganas'.

The Kushiluv also performed dance-drama productions by forming a family troupe (from skilled members of their own family).

Many of them wandered around alone as 'Hari-Katha' singers and sang the glories of the Lord. They parallelly used to perform and teach yoga.

A few others provided their performing art skills as a source of entertainment and danced for the royal courts and in the homes of rich merchants.

Some from the Kushiluv community pondered upon, expanded and wrote *'Shastra'* texts related to dance and created new texts as well. These scholarly pursuits allowed them to further the concepts of *'prayoga'* or practice as directed by Sage Bharata. They used to conceptualize new forms of Karanas, Angharas, Chari, Sthana, Mandal, Gatis, and Hasta-Mudras (Hand gestures), keeping in mind the rules set by Bharata Muni.

The period after the 10th century marked the entry of foreign invaders and the beginning of Islamic civilization in India.

Epilogue by Kiran Java

Dr. Puru Dadheech believes that the roots of Kathak classical dance can be traced back to the Natyashastra treatise, a text which codifies the movements of the dance form. He believes that the dance form is as old as time itself and is eternal. The Natyashastra is considered one of the earliest and most comprehensive texts on the performing arts in ancient India, and its influence can still be seen in various forms of classical Indian dance today, including Kathak.

From the discussions in this book, we can see that the older treatises such as Bharata's Natyashastra

(1st century BC–3rd century AD), Nandikeshwar's Abhinaya Darpan (completed after Natyashastra), Matanga Muni's Brihaddeshi (5th century AD), Damodara Mishra in the Kuttini Mata (8th century), Rajasekhara in his Kavya Mimamsa (9th century), Abhinavagupta's Abhinava Bharati (11th century), Shrngadeva's Sangeet Ratnakar (13th century) among others, have dance termed as *Nritta* or *Nritya* as the case may be. (Note: The earliest texts do not refer to dance as *Nritya*; the word *Nritta* is used.)

The classical style names as we know them in the list of recognized 'classical' styles (Kathak, Kathakali, Manipuri, and Bharatnatyam and later the additions Kuchpudi, Odissi, Mohiniyattam and Sattriya) are not listed in the dance treatises of ancient India. According to the various texts, dance is referred to as Nrtta, Tandava, Nritya, Lasya, and so on.

It must be noted that Sharangadeva has mentioned the word 'Kathak' in his Sangeeta Ratnakara in verse 1348.

> kathaka bandidinashchatre vidyavantah priyamvadah
>
> *They are the kathaks, the reciters of 'stutis', the learned and the speakers skilled in the art of speaking well, are knowledgeable in the presentation of 'kavya.*

(See: Leela Venkataraman, Review of Kathak Lok in the online dance magazine Narthaki.com. September 6, 2022)

Another point of view is that Kathak emerged

as a dancing community and then was assigned to Kathak dance. In the 'Introduction' section of her book titled Kathak, Dr. Shovana Narayan too agrees and has mentioned:

> *'the practice of male devotional dancers had always existed' and 'the temple dancing tradition by women became prominent from the 4th century AD"*

(See Kathak. 2012. Shubhi Publications).

An article in the Hindustan Times of 15th March 1937 mentions Kathak as the name of this dance style for the first time. The same article also supports the theory that there was a community named Kathak who performed and taught dance.

In his book on Sanskrit Drama, Arthur Berriedale

Keith (1879-1944) distinguishes two types of Kathak.

> Dharakas who recite mantras and use gestures to communicate the message (the performer Kathaks), and Pathaks, who recite mantras but only narrate stories from ancient texts.
>
> (See Narayan, & Mishra. (2008). The Historicity of "Dharaka" Kathak. Sangeet Natak Journal, XLII Number2.)

The origin story of dance is also discussed, where Shiva asks Sage Bharata to include dance in the Purvaranga of his dramas. This is described on page 59 of Ghosh (2016) Chaukhamba Surbharati Prakashan, Natyasastram: Vol. I.

On Page 1095, Ghosh describes the descent of drama in which Bharata accepts Raja Nahush's request and sends his sons to Earth (2016). Chaukhamba Surbharati Prakashan, Natyasastram: Vol. II.

The discussion's main takeaway is that Kathak dance has always existed. There should be no confusion or fallacies about Kathak being a Mughal-era dance. We've also learned that the dance has been named Kathak after the community (of the same name) that performed it. We've seen various *shlokas* (verses) on Kathak and dance in general, as well as creation stories. We have seen a long list of activities carried out by the Kushilava and others in order to propagate and expand the dance form and become the sole torchbearers of this dance from the beginning of time to the 10th century.

I'd like to thank Mahamahopadhyaya Dr. Puru Dadheech for sharing his valuable insights into the origins of Kathak classical dance. I look forward to continuing this discussion on the development of Kathak in the next part of the book, "Journey of Kathak Part 2: In Conversation with Dr. Vibha Dadheech and Dr. Puru Dadheech".

If you've enjoyed this book, please leave a review on Amazon or Goodreads so that more readers can learn about the true story of the journey of Kathak.

Thank you.

Reference Shlokas

Shloka - Mahabharata

kathakAshachApare rAjan shramanasha

cha vanaukasa: divyAkhyAnAni ye

chApi paThanti madhurama dvijA:

(Mahabharata Adiparva, 1: 206: 3)

(ITRANS transliteration)

With the king on the way to the forest were

the kathakas, pleasing to the eyes and ears

as they sang and narrated sweetly.

Narayan, S. (2016, December 27). A Quick Introduction To Kathak And The Debate Surrounding It. Swarajyamag.

kathakAshachApare rAjan

shramanasha cha vanaukasa:

(Mahabharata - 1/251/3)

(ITRANS transliteration)

Dadheech, P., & Dadheech, V. (2009). *Nritya Nibandh*. Bindu Prakashan Publication.

Shloka – Origin of dance

mayapidam smritam

nrittam sandhyaakaaleshu

nrityata nanakaranasamyuktairan-

gaharairvibhushitam purvarangavidhavasmin

tvaya samyak prayujyatam

(Natyashastra Chapter 4 Verse 13)

Now in the evening, while performing it, I remembered that dance made beautiful by Angaharas consisting of different Karanas. You may utilize these in the Preliminaries (Purvaranga) of a play.

Ghosh. (2016). *Natyasastram: Vol. I.*

Chaukhamba Surbharati Prakashan.

Shloka - Descent of Drama on Earth

King Nahusha Approaches Bharata

proktavaamshca tato mam tu

nripatih sa kritaanjalih

idamicchami bhagavan

natyamurvyaam pratishithatam

(Natyashastra Chapter 36 Verse 58)

Then the king with joined palms said to me, 'Revered sir, I should like to see this dramatic performance established on earth.

Ghosh. (2016). *Natyasastram: Vol. II.* Chaukhamba Surbharati Prakashan.

Shloka - Occasions for dance

vivahaprasa vavahapramodabhyudayadisu

vinodakaranam ceti nrittametatpravartitam

(Natyashastra Chapter 4 Verse 267)

Weddings, birth ceremonies, and such other

auspicious occasions that require merriment, are

occasions that require dance to be performed.

yasminnange prasadam tu grihiyannayika

kramat tatah prabhritti nrittam

tu sesesvangesu yojayet

(Natyashastra Chapter 4 Verse 316)

All occasions of joy call for the use of dancers performing Nritta sequence.

Narayan. (2002). Kathak. Shubhi Publications.

Shloka - Sangeet Ratnakar

Kathaka bandinashcanye

vidyavantaha priyamvadah

prashansa kushalashcanye

caturah sarvamatushu

Kathaks, composers and the learned

are intelligent, speak sweetly, and

use their skills for praise.

(Sangeeta Ratnakara, 13th CE)

Mishra, & Narayan. (2008). Historicity of Dharaka Kathak. *Sangeet Natak, XLII*(2), 6.

Shloka - Harshacharitam

Bhratarau

parashavauchandrasenamatrishenau,

bhashakavirishanah, mardangikojimootaha,

gayanausomilagrahadityau kurangika, ...

vanshikau madhukaraparavatau,

gandharvaupadhyayo durdurakaha.

samvahika keralika, lasakyuva tandavikaha,....

shailaliyuva shikhandikaha, nartaki

harinika... kathako jayasenaha, ... danduriko

damodaraha, aindrajali kashcakorakshaha,

maskari tamracudakaha.

He was accompanied by the twins, Chandrasena

and Matrisen, Bhasha poet Ishan, ...

mridanga player Jimuta, singers Somila and Grihaditya, stylist Kurangika, ... flautists Madhukara and Paravat, music teacher Guru Durduraka, feet masseur Keralika, graceful dancer Tandavika,... actor-dancer Shikhandaka, lady dancer Harinika, ... Kathak Jayasena, player of 'durdura' instrument Damodara, magician Chakoraksha and jester Tamracuda.

(Harshacharitam, 6th AD, Chapter 1)

Mishra, & Narayan. (2008). Historicity of Dharaka Kathak. *Sangeet Natak, XLII*(2), 5-6

Shloka - Prakrit verse

maggasira suddha pakkhe nakhhate

varanastye nayartye uttarapuratthime

disibhage garjgaye mahanadiye tat e savvo

kathaka bhingaranatenam tise stuti kayam

yehi raya adinaho bhavenam passayi...

(Prakrit verse, Asokan-Brahmi

script, 4th century BC)

In the month of magha, in the period of

shukla paksha nakshatra, to the north of

Varanasi, on the banks of the Ganges, the

shringara dance of the Kathaks in praise of the

Almighty (stuti) pleased Lord Adinatha...

(English translation of the Prakrit Text)

Manuscript Library, Kameshwar Singh

Darbhanga Sanskrit University, Darbhanga,

Bihar. Courtesy: Kamal Kishor Mishra

Mishra, & Narayan. (2008). Historicity of

Dharaka Kathak. Sangeet Natak, XLII(2), 4.

Shloka - Constant Prayoga

evam natyaprayoge bahuvidhivihitam

karmashaastrapranitam na proktam

yacca lokadanukritikaranaat

samvibhaavyam vidhijnaih

kincanyat sasyaipurnaa bhavatu

vasumati shaashvato nashtaroga

santirgobraahmanaanaamam

narapatiravanim paatu cemaam samagraama

(Natyashastra Chapter 36 Verse 83)

Thus, many practices sanctioned by Shastras have been described in connection with the performance of dramas. Whatever remains unmentioned should be included into practice by experts from/by observing people in the world.

Ghosh. (2016). *Natyasastram: Vol. II.* Chaukhamba Surbharati Prakashan.

Reference - Amarakosha

kushIlava puM|

kAthikaH

samAnArthaka:chAraNa,kushIlava

shailAlinastu shailUShA jAyAjIvAH

kRRishAshvinaH | bharatA ityapi

naTAshchAraNAstu kushIlavAH ||

vRRitti : vAkyavistarakalpanA

(ITRANS transliteration)

Reference - Kalpadruma

shailUShaH, puM, shilUShasyApatyamiti

shilUSha + aN naTaH |

dhUrttaH | tAladhArakaH | iti shabdaratnAvalI ||

(ITRANS transliteration)

Books By This Author

Meeting The Kathak Rishi: A Brief Interaction With Mahamahopadhyaya Dr. Puru Dadheech's Kathak Research

This is a very short read that describes my tryst with Kathak classical dance and its Shastras, how I met Mahamahopadyay Dr. Puru Dadheech, and the doors to a wonderful world that opened up. This short read contains excerpts from my previously published articles about Mahamahopadyay Dr. Puru Dadheech's work that have been enjoyed by readers. These are but a few pearls from the ocean of knowledge that have been researched and shared by Mahamahopadhyay Dr. Puru Dadheech and my interaction with his research. If you are a reader who takes joy in reading about Kathak or are curious about its Shastras then this short read is for you.

The Sacred Love Letter: Krishna Weds Rukmini

The Sacred Love Letter is the story of the first love letter received by Krishna, the darling of Braja. It has been sent by Princess Rukmini of the Kingdom of Vidarbha. The book narrates why the Princess of

Vidarbha has to secretly send a letter to Krishna, the contents of her message of love, and Krishna's heroic response.

Let There Be Calamities : 26 Ways Queen Kunti Praised Krishna

The Mahabharata war has just ended. Yudhishthira, the eldest Pandava is seated on the throne of Hastinapura. But even after the war has ended, danger still persists for the Pandavas. This book shares some of those untold tales - how Krishna helps Arjuna subdue Drona's son, the murderer of the Pandava children, how he saves the unborn child of Uttara, the daughter-in-law of Arjuna, and how he advises the Pandavas at every step of the way. As Krishna prepares to return to Dwarka, he is approached by Queen Kunti who prays to him for calamities in her life. She has figured out that whenever danger is present in their lives, Krishna is by their side. She extols Krishna's glories and praises him in 26 different ways.

About The Author

Kiran Java

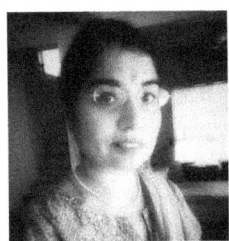

Kiran Java is known for her books on sacred writings (The Krishna Series) and her articles on Kathak Classical dance. She has over 20 years of experience in PR in the Middle East and her work is published by national and international media. She is curator-editor at Pushtimarg Studies and the host of the 'Krishna Stories with Kiran Java' Podcast.

She has a Masters degree in Mass Communication and Journalism and a B.Sc. degree in Marketing from Eastern Connecticut State University, USA. She has a certification in Vallabh Vedanta from Mumbai University and is pursuing a Post Graduate Diploma in Comparative Mythology.

Kiran holds a Diploma in Natyashastra with Kathak relevancy under Dr. Puru Dadheech and has learned Kathak classical dance under Dr. Nandkishore Kapote. She has learned Haveli Sangeet from Pt. B.P. Gandharva, and has released a few singles.

www.ingramcontent.com/pod-product-compliance
Lightning Source LLC
Chambersburg PA
CBHW050251220526
45465CB00002B/631